CANNIBAL

Written and photographed by

JAMES L. ANDERSON

A.H. & A.W. REED

Sydney Melbourne Wellington Auckland

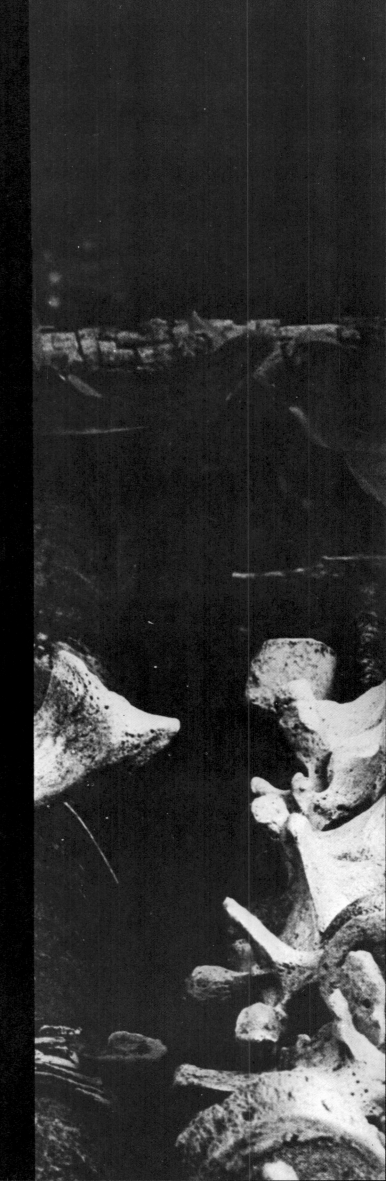

CANNIBAL

A PHOTOGRAPHIC AUDACITY

First published 1970

A. H. & A. W. REED

51 Whiting Street, Artarmon, Sydney
357 Little Collins Street, Melbourne
182 Wakefield Street, Wellington
29 Dacre Street, Auckland

SBN 589 07082 7

Reproduction prints by Graphic Images, Sydney
Set in Optima by Dalley Typesetters, Sydney
Printed and bound by Kyodo Printing Co, Tokyo

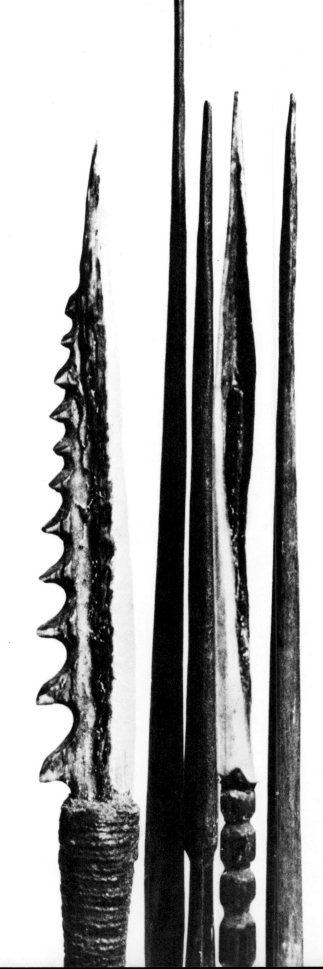

Produced by
CREATIVE PROJECTS
INTERNATIONAL PTY LTD
SYDNEY

Editors:
JILLIAN STEWART
RAYMOND HALL

Designed by
WILLIAM MOBBS

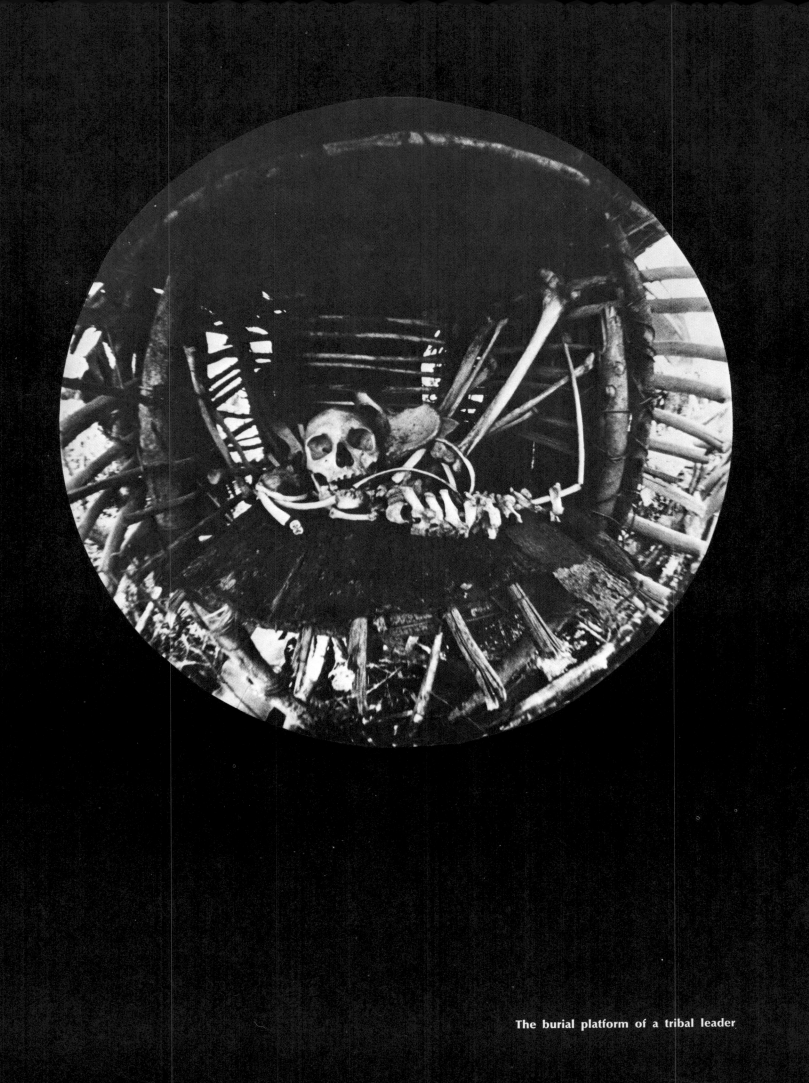

The burial platform of a tribal leader

Patrol Officer Alan Johnston and Darris
Wells at work in the Biami tribal area

Dedicated to all Patrol Officers
throughout the Territory of
Papua and New Guinea

CONTENTS

AUTHOR'S NOTES

It is seldom that a free-lance photo-journalist has the opportunity of recording in pictures and in words such dynamic and exciting material as contained in CANNIBAL. For this opportunity I wish to express my sincere thanks to the Administration of Papua/New Guinea and to the numerous Government officials both in Port Moresby and in the Western District. Without their help and co-operation this book would not have been possible.

This project was a real test for my photographic and recording equipment which had to stand up to extreme tropical conditions, rain, mud, and constant humidity. On numerous occasions during the trek various pieces of equipment were accidently dropped and bashed about by the carriers. However, all of the equipment stood up extremely well, which was proof beyond doubt of its durability.

The equipment used was as follows: three Nikon F camera bodies, one Nikkormat FTN camera body, one Nikon SP half-frame camera, one Widelux camera, a complete set of Auto Nikkor lenses ranging from 28mm to 200mm, one 21 mm f4 lens, one 500mm Nikkor Reflex f5 lens, one 55mm Auto Micro Nikkor lens, one Cosmos fisheye lens, one Mecablitz electronic flash unit with two Mecablitz extension heads, one Gossen Lunasix 3 exposure meter, one Gossen Sixtino exposure meter, two Nikkon electric motor drives with self-contained and separate battery packs, and one Akai XV portable stereo tape recorder. Meopta enlargers were used exclusively in the production of the black and white reproduction prints. I wish to express my thanks to R. Gunz (Photographic) Pty Ltd, Maxwell Photo-Optics Pty Ltd, Photographic Industrial Communications Systems, and Akai (Australia) Pty Ltd for their assistance in supplying equipment.

Special thanks are extended to Ansett Airlines of Australia, Ansett Airlines of Papua and New Guinea and to Qantas Airways for their support, and to Patrol Officer Darris Wells for his help and co-operation far beyond the call of duty.

I hope that you find as much excitement in reading CANNIBAL as I found in producing it.

JAMES L. ANDERSON

INTRODUCTION

The Cessna 172 droned on like a giant blowfly on the windowpane of cloudless sky, almost deafening from where I sat on the floor, cramped unceremoniously between patrol boxes of camping and photographic gear, bundles of frozen meat, cases of beer, a battered old mail sack and two bags of cement. I thought perhaps I should be sporting a sticker on my forehead stating 'This Side Up'. Above my head, between the cargo and the roof, were wedged several sheets of corrugated iron.

Below, and only partly visible through the small window, the all-engulfing, seemingly impenetrable green sea of jungle: a hopeless tangle of vines and trees that strangles the very life from the sun before it can caress the soil. I thought of this flat, swampy land, a wall-to-wall carpet of defiance stretching hundreds of miles from the Gulf of Papua to the Highlands of New Guinea, and pondered the fate of the many other small planes, like ours, that had crashed, barely bruising the walls of this green hell as they were swallowed. The jungle leaves no tombstones. It quickly covers its victims with a green shroud.

This was my fourth trip to New Guinea as a freelance photographer-writer and it would, I hoped, provide me with enough material to complete my book, 'New Guinea'.

I needed a coverage of the more primitive areas where, it was claimed, there were still cannibals who had never seen a white man. In a Port Morseby hotel, two weeks previously, a journalist friend had suggested Nomad Patrol Post. It sounded like a winner, and next day I paid the District Officer a visit to gather more information. I told him I wished to accompany a patrol out of Nomad, and showed him my credentials, explaining at the same time my book project. Although at first reluctant, he finally agreed to radio the District Officer at Daru, Western District Headquarters. Two weeks later a cable came through from Nomad with news that a patrol would be leaving in three days, and that I was welcome to tag along.

Next day I caught the scheduled flight to Daru and discussed my plans with the Acting District Commissioner; at this stage I knew little about Nomad except that cannibalism still existed in the area. The briefing by the Acting District Commissioner proved more than interesting, and left me wondering what I had let myself in for.

Until a few years ago, the white man knew little of the Biami area in the

Left: Patrol Officer Bill Patterson examines skull from tribal leader's burial platform

Overleaf: Acting Assistant District Commissioner Darris Wells demonstrates the White Man's weapon to primitive Biami tribesmen

Western District. In November 1962, Acting Assistant District Officer M. Lang and Patrol Officer R. W. Henderson took a patrol into the middle reaches of the Strickland River. One member of the patrol, Constable Kasiga, was hacked to death by four natives who claimed he had assaulted one of their wives. After investigating the killing, the Administration set up the Nomad Patrol Post that same year. Then, in May 1967, when it seemed that relations with the natives in surrounding areas had improved, the Kubor cannibals made a dawn attack only twelve miles from Nomad station. They swept in with their deadly clubs and bone-tipped arrows and slaughtered four people as they slept in a village longhouse. Two of the bodies were carved up on the spot, and carried off to be eaten.

Shortly after, a missionary patrol ventured into the area and the Administration became worried that their presence might stir up the Biami people still further. Alan Johnson, Patrol Officer from Nomad, went into the area with ten policemen to establish the Obeimi Base Camp. For the next two years Johnson had the tiresome and, at times, seemingly hopeless task of convincing these primitive people that the Administration was there to help them. With so few men, and limited financial support, his efforts had much less effect than he had hoped. Director of District Administration, Mr T. W. Ellis, has a staff of only 520. There are not enough patrol officers and district commissioners to go round. The smaller communities like Nomad suffer. The Acting District Commissioner explained that Administration was aware of, and concerned about, the situation in the Biami area. With the rest of the territory developing so rapidly, forgotten pockets like the Nomad area could become political dynamite in a few years.

As I left the District Office, the Acting District Commissioner called

Details of burial platform of the tribal elders　　　　　19

after me, 'By the way, Anderson, do you have a gun?'

'Yes,' I replied, 'I organised a .45 pistol and permit before leaving Port Moresby.'

'Good,' he said, 'but just remember that while you're at Nomad, you're to follow orders from Officer Wells. Let him know about the gun as soon as you arrive. You may carry it only with his permission, even though you have a permit.'

I found accommodation that night with the Catholic mission in Daru and the following morning talked to Officer Wells by radio from District Headquarters. He confirmed arrangements for me to accompany the patrol, and gave me a strange list of things to bring which, at the time, made little sense to me. Included on the list were dieselene, calico, razorblades, salt, a special type of leech repelent, extra socks and long trousers (for the tropics?!), plus a few cheap hunting knives, axes, and a couple of bottles of whisky. At least I knew what the whisky was for.

By now we were banking sharply to the right and I glanced out hoping for a sign of life, but still the green, forbidding jungle stretched out before my eyes like a huge sheet of blotting paper ready to absorb us without trace. Then, suddenly, and with a jolt, we were bouncing along a grassy landing strip, and in the distance I could see a tin shack with the word 'Nomad' painted roughly above the front door. A few yards in front of the shack stood a group of scruffy natives, some dressed in shorts and a shirt, others in lap-laps or arse-grass. As we bounced to a halt, three Europeans strolled up and started opening the cargo hatch and door.

I stumbled out, stretched, and looked around. So this was Nomad . . .

20   **Traditional carving on Biami arrow shafts**

NOMAD

A short stocky man, about five feet two inches, broad-shouldered, with a bushy moustache and looking disturbingly like a South American dictator, stepped forward and shook my hand.

'Darris Wells,' he said by way of introduction. 'You must be the mad photographer who's supposed to be going on patrol with us. Must say you do look fitter than I imagined.' He turned and introduced me to Alan Johnson and Bill Patterson. Johnson was rather tall and lean, with an immaculately-kept beard, blue eyes and wavy hair. Patterson, although not fat, appeared immense, his big-boned frame standing more than six feet six inches tall.

I pitched in and helped unload the plane and, after throwing on board a few bundles of pawpaw and pineapple for Daru, the pilot taxied off and the small plane was soon roaring down the strip in front of us. As it lifted off, the group of natives around us pointed and chattered excitedly.

'If we had planes coming in every day,' explained Darris, 'we'd never get any bloody work done. But with only one plane a fortnight, it's a bit of a treat for the natives.'

Patterson turned and said, 'I think the wife's got the coffeepot on. How about a cuppa?'

Everyone agreed and we strolled off towards a neat little European-style house a few hundred yards away. As we moved off, Darris shouted to the natives over his shoulder, 'Kisim cargo i go long opis.' They were already gathering everything that had arrived on the plane.

As we walked along the track leading to the house and a group of other buildings, Darris explained the set-up: 'This is the football field we're walking across now, and the two little houses over there belong to Alan and me, and Bill and his wife. The group of thatch-roofed houses on the left include the office, medical aid post, post office, radio shack, and storehouse. Down there at the other end of the strip, the big native-style house with the barbed-wire fence is the calabuse, and on past there the small iron-roofed houses belong to the police. The building to the right of the police houses is the Buyers Club.'

'Buyers Club?' I asked.

'Yes. The police boys, clerks, interpreters and ourselves formed the club so as to save money on supplies. The club buys in large quantities, then resells at a very nominal profit. The profits are then used to better conditions on the station, such as improve the football field, volley ball nets, and other items not normally furnished for us by Administration.'

I pointed out that for so few buildings they seemed spread over an unusually large area.

'If we had planes coming in every day . . .
we'd never get any bloody work done'

. . . with a bushy moustache and looking disturbingly like a South American dictator . . .

'Yes,' said Darris, 'the reason is that in the initial stages of establishing a patrol post, the buildings are spread out, making an attack and takeover of the entire post more difficult. Also, by clearing a large section of land at the beginning, it's easier for the patrol post to grow over the years. Another advantage, of course, is in mosquito and leech control. They love the jungle, and once the land is cleared you don't have too much trouble from them. Walk a hundred yards into the bush at the end of the strip, and you'll be covered with leeches. But you'll find out all about that when we go on patrol.'

As we approached Bill Patterson's house, a small freckle-faced redhead waved to us from the verandah. At her feet a fourteen-month-old child played with an empty powdered-milk can. Cases of canned meat blocked the stairs to keep the baby from falling. 'Come in and meet the family, Jim,' said Bill. 'This is my wife Jill and our son David.'

Jill smiled and said, 'Come in boys, coffee's almost ready.' The house was extremely tidy, with a sprinkling of formica-topped and plastic-covered furniture here and there. I immediately wondered how an attractive young mother like Jill felt living in a place like this. Somewhere along the line I had gathered the idea that Nomad was a single man's station. We sat around the table, and Jill brought out a plate of freshly-baked scones and poured coffee. I remarked on the loneliness of the station and its obvious disadvantages for a married couple with a young child.

'It's not too bad,' said Bill. 'We had two years in Port Moresby when we first came up here, and we both hated it. Next we were stationed on a lonely mountain-top patrol post near Tari, in the Southern Highlands. This was much more to our liking, and when it came time for transfer we asked to be stationed in a remote area again. You see, in the bigger, more established towns in New Guinea you still have the disadvantages of irregular transport and food supply, and little entertainment, but you don't have the advantages of being completely away from it all and being able to do more or less what you want, as long as you perform your job well. We've only been here for a month, having just come back from leave in Sydney, but so far we feel we're going to like it.'

Jill stirred her coffee and remarked, 'It worries me sometimes, thinking what I would do if the baby was seriously ill. It could be anything up to three days before a plane could get in to fly us to the nearest hospital at Daru. But we're very lucky with David, he's always been such a healthy baby. And we do have a good selection of medical supplies here on the station. The one thing I can't get used to is not having fresh vegetables. In the highlands we had more than we could eat. But I guess the abundance of pawpaw and pineapple makes up for it a bit. We've already started planting a vegetable garden on the riverbank at the back of the house, so by next year we should be all right.'

When we'd finished our coffee, Darris took me to the house where he and Alan lived. It was identical to Bill's but far less tidy—the lack of a woman's hand in the house was noticeable at first glance. Darris showed me to an empty bunk and told me to unpack and make myself comfortable.

'When you've got yourself organised, you can wander down to the office and I'll give you a rundown on the patrol we'll be making.'

Later that afternoon he pulled out maps of the area and told me more about the Biamis. One of his first questions was, 'Do you have a gun?'

I told him I did, and also mentioned what the ADC at Daru had said.

'With any luck, you won't have to use it. But personally I wouldn't think of going into the Biami area without being fully armed. I'll feel much better knowing that you are, too.'

He went on: 'The object of our patrol is to investigate two reported raids

One of the thatch-roofed huts on the outskirts of Nomad Patrol Post

in the Biami area. You never know about these reports until you look into the facts for yourself: it could be an enraged husband who has axed his wife for disobedience, or a small skirmish between two groups over land, with possibly a few people merely wounded by the odd arrow; or it could be a cannibalistic raid with a dozen or more people killed and eaten.

'What we have to do is find out exactly what did happen and, depending upon its seriousness, arrest those involved and take the necessary legal action. "Necessary legal action" may sound a bit strange to you, but what we have to do is to strike a happy medium between conventional European law and whatever will have the best overall effect on the villagers as a whole. For example, the law usually demands life imprisonment for premeditated murder. On the other hand, killing, and a law even older than ours—"an eye for an eye, a tooth for a tooth"—are part of the Biamis' everyday life. If I arrest a villager for murder and we sentence him to twenty years or life imprisonment, the other villagers will think we have taken him away for food. On the other hand, particularly when there has been only brief contact made with a village, and where the natives are still unsure of the Government's attitude and power —in fact what the Government really is —by charging the villager with riotous behaviour and sentencing him to six months in jail at one of the bigger stations, such as Daru or Kiunga, we give him the opportunity to see that the Government consists of more than just one or two patrol officers. He sees that it consists of (in his eyes) hundreds of Europeans with many houses and buildings, strange machines called automobiles, water that comes out of strange-looking things on the wall— things he or his people never dreamed existed.'

'But, Darris,' I said, 'how can you

'By sentencing a villager to six months jail . . . he is given the opportunity to see that the government consists of more than just one or two patrol officers.'

27

charge a man with riotous behaviour, when he has committed first-degree murder, and still be within the bounds of the law?'

'Easy. The defendants in most cases have eaten the evidence. And without a body and positive identification, it's difficult to prove murder. The European law works both for and against us. After serving six months in jail in a place like Daru, the man will be sent back to his people, and will be looked upon by them as a great man. He will bring back knowledge and tales of the outside world, and will also have learned either Pidgin or Motu and, with any luck, possibly even a little English. This means the next time we are on patrol in the area we'll have far less trouble communicating with the natives.

'The other problem that arises, is that the villagers often refuse to believe one man's tales of the outside world. Therefore, if at all possible, we try to grab at least three or four people involved in a particular raid and sentence them all to six months' jail. The exact sentence, of course, depends on how much contact we've had with the particular village, and the exact circumstances leading to the raid or murder. A minimum sentence is usually six months, but in some cases it's as much as five years.'

The office in which we were sitting was large and airy, and made from bamboo and other local materials. A large tarpaulin had been stretched across the rafters above Darris's desk to keep out dust and bits of thatch-roof. In each corner were bundles of bone-tipped arrows, confiscated on previous patrols, and a large number of stone axes and fighting clubs hung from the walls. Decorated tortoise-shells and other artifacts were also scattered around the room.

While I browsed through these relics of death, Darris finished off the day's work with instructions to his police sergeant for the following day's road work detail. It was now near five o'clock, and Darris suggested we take a quick walk around the station before returning to his place for a cold beer.

As we walked past the Buyers Club and turned towards the river, I spotted a suspended bridge, made from vines that stretched about twenty feet above the water. And just behind the patrol post was a huge cut in the river bank which appeared to have been made by a bulldozer.

A group of natives were dragging old sheets of iron-roofing up and down the riverbank with stones and earth piled on them. Just as I was about to ask Darris what was happening, Alan came up from the riverbank shouting, 'What do you think of our new road, Jim?'

'What road?' I asked.

'Don't be insulting, mate. I've been working on this bloody road for just on six weeks now. I realise this cut in the riverbank could have been done in two hours with a bulldozer, but how would you put one of those things on a Cessna? Our strip is only Cat. D rating, which means we can't even bring in a DC3.

I looked in amazement. 'You mean all that earth has been moved in little piles on iron roofing?'

'That's right, mate. Mind you, once we finish this grade and cross the river, it'll be a lot easier cutting the road through the flat jungle. We'll have a large raft floating on forty-four-gallon oil drums to take the Landrover back and forth across the river. That means that once the road is finished we can drive about thirty miles into the jungle and patrol quite a number of villages along the way. Mind you, we don't have a Landrover yet, but once we have a road, Administration will have to supply us with some type of vehicle.'

'But where does the road go?'

Right: Darris finished off the day's work with instructions to his police sergeant . . .

Overleaf: The road to nowhere

'Nowhere, really. It'll end up at a small mission station about thirty miles from here. With the road down, we'll be able to go out on patrol once a week and bring the area under total control much quicker than we could with our monthly patrols on foot.'

The three of us walked towards the jail and police quarters at the end of the football field, Alan and Darris discussing the patrol on which we were about to embark. It was decided that Alan would stay behind to run the patrol post, giving Darris an opportunity to familiarise Bill with the area.

'How much gear do you want to take with you?' Alan asked.

'Well, I've got about four patrol boxes,' I said. 'It's mostly photographic and recording equipment, but I can cut it down to two if I have to.'

'Not to worry,' said Darris, 'we'll be taking between sixty and seventy carriers with us and, if I remember correctly, you've got two one-man and two two-man patrol boxes?'

'That's right.'

'Well, that's only six carriers for your gear—not enough to be concerned about.'

'How many police boys do you want to take?' asked Alan.

Darris paused for a moment to think. 'If I leave you with about four, will that be enough?'

'Sure,' said Alan.

'Good, that means we can take twelve on patrol. If I have time after I clear up this trouble at Nefolifi and Mogulubi, we'll rest up for a few days at base camp, and then try to make our way down to the Rentoul River. I know there are several villages down there that haven't yet been contacted, and it should make interesting material for Jim. I spotted them from the air a few weeks ago. There are at least two quite large villages.'

'One of the problems we have in this area Jim,' he said, turning to me, 'is that the villagers are constantly on the move. What they do is plant gardens on a new site while living and eating from their old gardens. By the time these are exhausted, the new ones, which may be four or five miles away, have started to produce and so they move their village to the new site. Trouble is, they change their village name when they move, and then start planting gardens at yet another location. We haven't yet been able to determine exactly how long they stay on one site, but it seems to be about a year to eighteen months. You can imagine the problems this gives us in mapping, and also in determining exactly which villages have been contacted and which haven't.'

As we approached the barbed-wire fence surrounding the jail, something that sounded like a miniature helicopter swooped past my head. I ducked— and Darris and Alan both began to laugh. 'Don't worry,' said Alan, 'it's only a hornbill. It's a pet of one of the police boys.'

I looked at the flimsy jail and remarked to Darris, 'Surely even a five-year-old would have little trouble getting out of there?'

'That's right. But we seldom have that problem, because most of the prisoners are from villages miles from here. If they escape, their chances of making it back to their villages are pretty slim. To get there, they'd have to pass through the tribal grounds of their traditional enemies. Any native who wanders around the jungle on his own outside his tribal area is fair game for the evening meal. The only time villagers wander out of their own area is in large groups, prepared for a fight.'

We strolled back to the house about six, settled down for a beer and, after a couple of hours of light conversation, turned in.

We had a big day ahead of us.

Left: . . . sounded like a miniature helicopter . . .

Overleaf: We were up at daybreak next morning checking supplies, carriers and equipment . . .

33

34

ON PATROL

We were up at daybreak next morning, checking supplies, carriers, and equipment, in preparation for the long patrol through the jungle. At eight o'clock we started out in single file down the airstrip: Darris Wells, Bill Patterson, myself, two interpreters, a medical orderly, a cook boy, twelve policemen and seventy-two carriers.

Just as we entered the thick sago swamp at the end of the airstrip, I looked back and saw the end of the carrier line reaching back to the football field, close to half a mile away.

It seemed only minutes before the leeches became aware of our presence. The repulsive little bloodsuckers were like Mexican jumping beans, flopping end-over-end up my boots and pants legs. Thank God for the long trousers! But soon we left the swamp and got on to a fairly good bush track, that made the going much easier. About an hour and a half out of Nomad we arrived at the village of Dfelomosom, in the Gubusi area, and while resting here and waiting for the rest of the patrol to catch up with us, Bill checked the village book and talked to the tribesmen through Nogoi, one of the interpreters.

After routine greetings were exchanged, we sat down in front of the long-house for a smoke and Darris began to tell me about Nogoi. 'A patrol officer found him wandering aimlessly in the jungle just over five years ago. His parents had been killed and eaten in a raid, so he was taken back to the patrol post and cared for by the station staff. Eventually he was trained to be a Government interpreter. Then, three years ago, following a major staff change at the post, Nogoi went back to his village and lived there for just over a year before coming back to Nomad to resume work as an interpreter. But we discovered recently that during his year of absence from the post he had gone with members of his village and revenged his parents' death by killing and eating those men who had devoured his parents three years before. This couldn't be definitely proved, though, and because he was such a good interpreter he was never charged. He has a sense of humour that is a real asset on patrol when it comes to keeping up morale. Some of the things he gets up to could be quite serious, but for some reason, when Nogoi is involved, they always end up being hilarious. On my last patrol I nicknamed him "the Comical Cannibal".'

We sat resting, and my thoughts wandered to the villagers crouched smiling around us. 'They seem glad to see us,' I remarked to Darris.

'With good reason. About nine months ago a group from the village of Gige raided this village and killed and ate two of the inhabitants. Four months ago

Overleaf, left: Soon we left the swamp and got on to a fairly good bush track . . .

Overleaf, right: . . . Bill checked the village book . . .

Left: On Patrol

37

Above: After routine greetings were exchanged . . .

Left: . . . they seemed glad to see us . . .

Right: . . . and revenged his parents' deaths . . .

the same thing happened, and another villager was killed and eaten. Three months ago we arrested one of the leaders from Gige, so the people from this village have begun to think of us as friends.'

We were soon on our way again, moving slowly through the undergrowth towards Gige. The jungle was fairly dry at this time of the morning and the walking easy, with only one or two small ridges to cross. At 12.30 that afternoon we stopped on a hillside just opposite Gige and prepared to make camp.

I had been an eager boy scout in my youth, but making camp on patrol was far from what I had expected. Three folding aluminium chairs were brought forward from the carrier line and set up beside us. We flopped thankfully into them, loosened our gunbelts, and lit up a smoke. Within seconds the bush became alive with activity. With the police supervising, the carriers cleared everything within one hundred yards, from big trees down to vines and dead leaves. What they couldn't chop down or pull out, they trampled flat.

Before we could finish our smokes, one of the patrol boxes was pushed in front of us to serve as a table, and the cook boy came forward with biscuits and hot coffee, which he had prepared on a nearby fire. I couldn't figure it out: it had always taken me at least an hour to boil water in the bush.

Three tents gradually began to take form. We took off our boots and got stuck into the leeches which had attached themselves to our ankles and legs. Even wearing long trousers and two pairs of socks, I still managed to find four. Darris and Bill, who wore shorts, had dozens of the stinking things clinging to them. They both claimed they would rather have the leeches than have to put up with the discomfort of long trousers in the hot, steamy climate, but, having never experienced the sensation of having

Right: . . . we took off our boots and got stuck into the leeches . . .

Far right: . . . folding aluminium chairs were brought forward . . .

42

Within seconds the bush became alive with activity

44

. . . complete with three welcome bedsleeves

dozens of bloodsuckers on my legs, I settled for being a bit hot and uncomfortable.

By the time we had our boots and socks off and finished our coffee, our tent had been erected, complete with three welcome bedsleeves. We retired to the tent, took off our sweat-soaked clothes, and changed into clean, dry shorts and a singlet. What a great feeling it is to expose your feet to the cool air after several hours' walking through rivers and mud, tangled tree roots and slippery boulders! Bare feet never felt so good. We stretched out on our bedsleeves, and Darris sent Nogoi to the village to tell them we needed food for our carriers, and wished to check the village book.

Darris then looked over at me and said, 'How would you like a nice hot shower, Jim?'

I laughed and said, 'Sure, with a beautiful maiden to scrub my back, of course.'

'Well I'm afraid you'll have to find your own maiden, but the hot shower is waiting,' said Darris, pointing to a small palm-frond enclosure a few yards away. I looked with amazement as the cook boy took off for the enclosure with a bucket of hot water from the fire. I grabbed a towel and followed. Inside the enclosure were two eight-foot posts with a rail stretching between them from which a canvas shower bucket was suspended. Small logs had been laid side by side to form a floor, and then covered with large green leaves (nice and soft on the sore feet). Two pieces of bamboo had been tied together to form a soap-dish on one side and there were several pegs for hanging clothes and a towel on. The whole enclosure was about six feet in diameter and private. Although fascinated by the facilities, I didn't stop to examine them; I was more intent on enjoying my hot shower. I returned to the tent and had another cup of

Left: . . . the hot shower is waiting

Above, left: . . . About twenty villagers appeared . . .

Right: . . . and was instructed to bring out the trade goods . . . cheap calico . . . matches and salt

coffee while the medical orderly attended my cuts, scratches, and leech bites. When Darris and Bill returned from their showers, they received similar treatment.

We had just settled back for a snooze when a loud chattering of excitement broke loose at the other end of the camp. About twenty villagers from Gige appeared before our tent with large quantities of bananas, taro, yams and breadfruit. Darris shouted for Nogoi, who soon appeared and was instructed to bring out the trade goods. Small twenty-cent Japanese hunting knives, cheap calico, razorblades, matches and salt. The salt, particularly, was in great demand and was traded by the handful. Darris later explained that it is the natives' form of candy or sweets, and that besides using it on their food, they eat it like sugar. They have no use for candy, or anything sweet that a patrol might offer them. The natives had also brought a medium-sized pig which Darris bought for the price of a small hatchet.

After checking the village book and making notation of our visit, we again traded with the villagers, this time for a few arrows, a club, and three stone axes. The villagers all seemed happy with their newly acquired goods and sat around the camp, shaving each other with razorblades and wrapping the bright red calico around themselves in various ways. Meanwhile, Darris arranged to have the pig cut up and after selecting a few choice pieces for us, divided the rest among the police and carriers. There wouldn't be much meat for the carriers by the time it was divided up, Darris told me, but with the exception of the odd can of meat or fish given to them by the Government, their main diet consists of bananas and kaukau. A few pieces of fresh pig now and then while on patrol give them extra energy for the heavy work they do during the day.

That night we dined on fresh pig, cooked in a pressure-cooker, jungle watercress, canned vegetables and pan-fried bread. Not bad, considering we were in the middle of one of the most primitive areas of the world. After downing a scotch, we hit the sack about eight o'clock, in preparation for the next day's walk.

At 4.30 we were up and having breakfast. The carriers and police had already started to break camp and we were on the track for Masamo village within an hour. Today's walk would be short, Darris told us, because he wanted plenty of time to investigate the reported incident at Masamo, which was less than two hours away.

We arrived there at about 7.30am and although the walk was fairly easy, Bill and I both felt the effects. Neither of us was as fit as Darris. Bill's two-month leave in Sydney had done him more harm than good.

Camp was erected in the same way as before, and Darris, Bill and I immediately went into the village with the interpreters and four policemen to investigate the reported incident. After the customary greetings and handshakes, we sat on the floor of the fighting platform, about twenty feet above the ground at the rear of the longhouse, and began inquiring into the reported trouble. Soon one of the men came forward and, through Nogoi, the following story evolved:

Just over two weeks ago three Mogulubi men arrived at our village. Our tribes are traditional enemies, and we were worried when they appeared with their clubs and axes. One of the visitors was the father of my wife. He spoke to me and said they had come in peace and would like to share food with us. I invited them into my house, and three elders of our village, myself, and the three Mogulubi men sat around the fire. We talked and ate. As the night went on everyone relaxed.

Suddenly a Mogulubi man jumped to his feet and struck one of our villagers

48

on the head with his axe. We ran for our clubs, but only one other man and myself escaped. They beat the other man to death with a stone club. We ran into the bush to get help from the other villagers sleeping in the garden houses.

When we returned to my house, only the intestines from my two friends lay on the bloodstained floor. The men from Mogulubi had cut up and shared the bodies before leaving. Since I had run, my wife's father took her and my young son back to Mogulubi. In the eyes of my wife's father, I am a coward. I tell you this only because I want my wife and son back. We will revenge the death of our people in our own way.

I listened intently as Darris cross-examined the man in an effort to get all the facts straight. We sat in a semi-circle, and a large bamboo pipe was passed for each to puff. The smoke was strong and pungent and one puff was more than enough for me. After more conversation and much persuasion, Darris convinced the Masamo man to accompany us the following morning in an effort to capture those involved in the raid. We would need his identification after the capture.

As we rose to leave, I spotted three burial platforms amidst the maze of chopped trees and spikes that formed the fortification surrounding the fighting platform. On each platform was a body, each at a different stage of decomposition. According to Darris the least decayed body had been dead about three weeks, the others about two months. He explained, 'The dead are put on to high platforms to prevent the rodents of the jungle from getting at the bodies. The women of the tribe then sit under the platforms for the first week or so and rub oils which drop from the bodies into their skin.'

'You'd think they'd all die of septicaemia,' I commented, 'what with all the cuts and scratches and leech bites they have—not to mention skin diseases.'

'They don't seem to have any trouble with it,' said Darris. 'They must have grown immune to it by now. What you have to be careful of, though, is shaking hands with the villagers when there are fresh bodies around, especially if you have any cuts or bites on your own hands. There's plenty of disinfectant in the first-aid kit, so be sure to scrub your hands well after any contact."

When we left, Darris led us along the opposite side of the house and underneath the fighting platform to within a few feet of the burial platforms. From a distance they hadn't looked so bad, but up close, with the repugnant smell of decaying flesh, it was all I could do to keep from retching. We returned to camp, and Darris began writing his report of the investigation.

Bill and I flopped into our bedsleeves and set about analysing the events of the morning. It was Bill's first patrol into the Biami, and the morning had been shattering for us both.

The sounds of the bird of paradise and various jungle creatures resounded around the campsite. After we'd finished lunch, I decided to bring out the tape recorder and attempt to capture the sounds on tape. I had been recording for almost an hour, and was about to finish, when I noticed a group of natives from the village, crouched on their heels nearby, watching intently. Each time I played back any of the sounds, the natives chattered and pointed at the 'white man's magical machine'.

I decided to have some fun with them and called Nogoi to help me. We then invited the group to sit around the tape recorder, while Nogoi started a brisk conversation with them in their own tongue. I left the recorder running, walked away a few yards and lit up a cigarette, pretending I wasn't using the machine.

Above, left: . . . the smoke was strong and pungent . . .

Left: As we rose . . . I spotted three burial platforms amidst the maze of chopped trees and spikes . . .

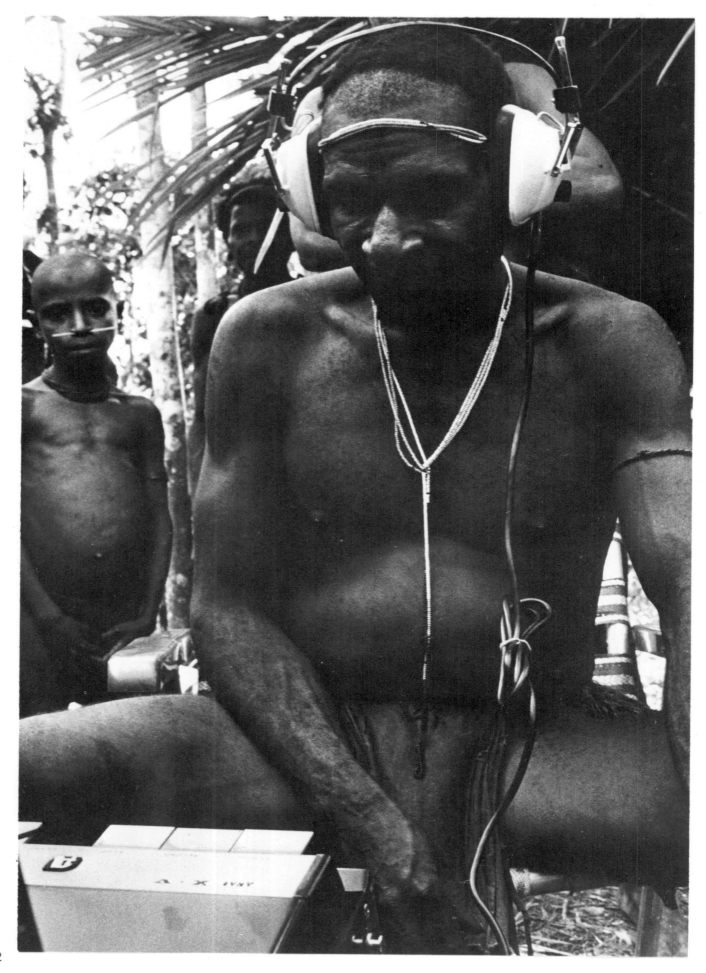

Left: This was the first time they had heard their own voices on tape . . .

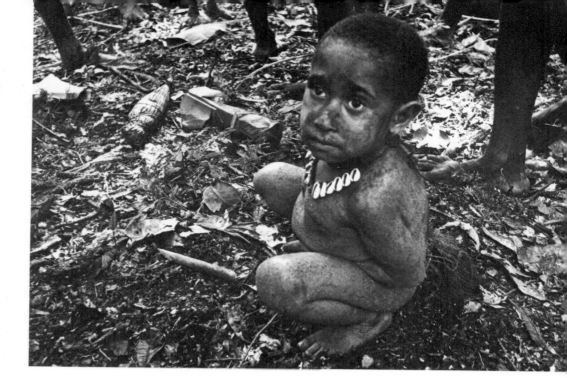

Right: Their reactions ranged from . . . indifference

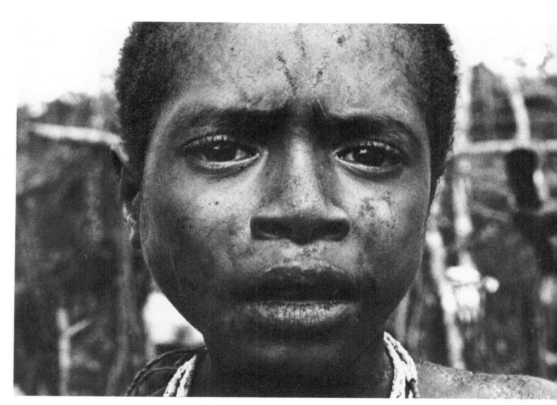

incomprehensibility

. . . being scared out of their wits

A few minutes later I walked back and rewound the tape. Then, so that I could capture each individual's reaction on film, I plugged in the earphones and placed them on the nearest villager's head. This was the first time they had heard their own voices on tape, and reactions ranged from indifference and incomprehensibility, to being scared out of their wits. One villager ripped the earphones off and ran for his life, fleeing so fast that he almost took the corner of the police tent with him. Two others were at first so petrified they couldn't move, but after they'd got used to the idea, they thought it was hilarious. The recording session lasted for almost two hours, but eventually I had to bring it to an end because of the drain on the batteries. As I put away the last of my equipment, Darris and Bill started setting up the radio gear. It was time to make afternoon contact with Alan at Nomad. We had been unable to reach him the first day out.

'Portable portable portable, Nomad Nomad Nomad, Portable Nomad, Portable Nomad,' Darris's voice rang out. A few more calls and some fine tuning on the radio dials, and Alan's voice came back: 'Nomad portable, Nomad portable, reading you loud and clear, what is your position?'

'We're at the village of Masamo, Alan. There's been a bit of a raid here from the Mogulubis. We're taking off about one in the morning with a witness from here, and will try to grab a few.'

'Roger Dee. Where will you camp tomorrow night, and when will I hear from you again? Over.'

'We'll have to go on to Base Camp tomorrow, Alan, to avoid any retaliation from the rest of the group. Over.'

'Roger. But what about Jim and Bill? That's a good fourteen-hour walk from where you are now.'

'Roger Dee. They'll just have to keep up the best they can. There are more than 200 in the Mogulubi group and I'm not about to get caught out in the bush by them when they're upset. Over.'

'Roger, Darris. Point taken. Call me from Base Camp as soon as you get there. No news for you here. Unless you have anything else, I'll say cheers now.'

'Roger, Alan. Cheers and out.'

I sat on a patrol box near the radio as the police boy started dismantling it. Fourteen hours, I thought to myself. Bill and I were exhausted after the two-hour walk this morning, not to mention the four-hour one the day before. Oh, well, I had asked to go on a Government patrol into a primitive region and that is exactly what I was doing. No use having second thoughts now. Just have to take the bad with the good, I told myself.

Nogoi tapped Darris on the shoulder and pointed to two villagers standing at the far end of the camp. One had mud and leaves plastered all over his foot.

'They want white man's medicine,' said Nogoi.

Darris grunted and told Nogoi to bring them over, then turned and called the medical orderly from the police boys' tent. We stood by and watched as the orderly started to scrape the dressing of leaves and mud from the native's foot. Twenty minutes later he got down to a gangrene mess almost as bad as we had seen on the burial platforms. From the centre of the wound he extracted a half-inch sliver of black palm. Besides being used for arrow tips, black palm spikes are placed around garden paths to discourage intruders. Either this fellow had been involved in an arrow fight, or had been poaching in someone else's garden.

Soon the wound was dressed and covered with clean white gauze. The native then proudly announced he had a stomach ache, and his friend claimed he had a headache, both with the help of Nogoi's interpretation, of course. An exasperated look came over Darris's face as he muttered, 'Oh, no, not again.'

I didn't understand at the time, but the reason for Darris's exasperation soon became apparent. The orderly brought out a king-sized bottle of castor oil and a can containing several hundred aspirins. As the two natives were treated for their respective ailments, at least fifty other men, women, and children appeared from all sides of the camp, all either rubbing their stomachs or holding their heads. They were told to form a queue. The orderly passed out two aspirin and a glass of water to each of the head-holders, and Darris gave each of the stomach-rubbers a tablespoon of castor oil. Forty-five minutes later the task was complete. Darris sighed and said, 'They've managed to develop medicine that's foul-tasting to us, so why can't someone develop a medicine that's foul-tasting to these people?'

It was now almost five o'clock and the cookie had hot water ready for our showers. Bill and Darris showered first, and by the time I had finished mine our evening meal was ready. Although not as good as the previous night's meal, the fried bananas, taro and yams complemented the canned beef stew quite well, and with the exception of a minor distraction halfway through, the meal was most enjoyable. Each night a number of carriers would congregate between the tent and cookhouse to ask for empty food cans, bottles, lids and boxes which they used for drinking cups and to decorate their hair.

Tonight, however, as I stuck my fork into a juicy piece of fried banana, I heard a funny crackling noise from just outside the tent. I looked up to see a carrier sitting cross-legged on the ground, a spider, with at least a six-inch leg span, stretched between both hands as he ripped it apart with his teeth. The spider was still kicking slightly.

'His evening meal?' I asked Darris.

'No,' said Darris, 'just a snack.'

With chow over, the three of us settled back in our bedsleeves with a scotch. The fire burned brightly a few yards away, and a hurricane lamp hung from the centre of the tent. I was curious to know why men like Darris and Bill chose this rough, isolated way of life and shunned a more comfortable and conventional one in Australia.

'Well,' said Darris, 'I was adopted from a Greek orphanage at the age of ten by an Australian couple. My father is a Rear Admiral in the Australian Navy, and I could easily have had a soft, cushy job down south. But that's not what I want out of life: I want to do something worthwhile, and be somebody—but on my own, without my folks' help.

'I reckon they did enough just bringing me to Australia and educating me. Now I want to show my appreciation by standing on my own two feet. I've been up here now for several years as a patrol officer and have just recently become acting Assistant District Commissioner. The work is satisfying, and I like being my own boss. I don't need the big cities, or a boss breathing down my neck eight hours a day.'

Bill joined the conversation: 'It's much the same for Jill and me. We can't stand big cities and all those bloody people. I hate waiting in queues and crowded department stores. Even if we do have to wait six months for some of our supplies, it's better than shopping in those crowded shops. It may be a bit awkward now with David being so young, but I reckon it'll be a lot better place to bring him up than Sydney or Melbourne.'

'Well, it's eight o'clock,' said Darris, 'and we've got to get up in five hours, so we'd better get some sleep. Tomorrow is going to be rough.'

THE CAPTURE

It was one o'clock in the morning when we broke camp. The moon was full, but most of the light was absorbed by the dense jungle. It had been raining, and moss-covered tree roots crisscrossed our path with treachery, causing us to stumble with almost every step. We came to a small river, about thirty feet across. A tree bridged the banks twenty feet above the water. Bill and Darris cautiously edged their way across, the flicker of their torches showing a ripple of water and tangled undergrowth beneath them.

Then it was my turn. The others had already disappeared into the bush on the far bank. I worked my way across, a few treacherous inches at a time. Midway, suddenly I lost my balance. I fell to my hands and knees; carefully I rose to my feet again, reached what I thought was the far bank, and stepped off the log. Nothing! My feet dangled helplessly in mid air as I grasped and desperately clung to the log by one arm. What had appeared to be solid ground was nothing more substantial than the tops of scrub and kunai grass growing high above the riverbed.

Bill appeared, his giant hand stretching out to pull me to safety. We continued on. Darris's torch flickered at the head of the patrol as he picked his way through the jungle. Nogoi slashed away at the vines in front. Six policemen, armed with .303 rifles, walked close behind me. So that they would not attract attention, the seventy-two carriers followed about fifteen minutes behind with an additional police guard bringing up the rear of the patrol.

It was 2.30 in the morning when we emerged from the jungle into a clearing. All foliage had been cut down on the hill that lay before us. Giant trees had been felled, one across the other, to form a tangled fortification. Saplings had been hacked down at irregular heights leaving dangerous spikes amongst the slippery logs. Primitive, perhaps, but effective. A small hut stood at the top of the hill, clearly visible in the moonlight.

The man from Masamo pointed to the hut. 'The father of my wife and his two companions live there. The main village of Mogulubi is two hours' walk away.'

We collapsed on a rotting log and lit up a smoke. Darris sent Nogoi back with instructions for the rest of the patrol. 'No noise, no torches.' Nogoi slipped away quietly.

The carriers had now caught up and grouped a few yards away in the bush. We walked back to where they waited, and Darris and Nogoi briefed them on surrounding the hut.

Soon we were edging our way up the hill, crawling along the wet, slippery

Left: '. . . had cut up and shared the bodies before leaving'   **Overleaf: A small hut stood at the top of the hill . . .**

logs, through the maze of spikes and tangled roots. We reached a spot a few yards from the hut and paused. The police and carriers slowly surrounded the house. Although the night was warm I shivered, knowing that at any moment, from a crack in the bamboo walls of the hut, a bone-tipped arrow might find its mark. I checked the pistol clutched in my hand.

Darris was suddenly shouting. 'Kwari! Mode! . . . Kwari! Mode!'

And we charged through the small log door into the darkened hut. Instant bedlam broke loose. Women and children screamed hysterically as the police crashed through the walls of the hut with their rifles. Carriers, armed with stout sticks, plunged through the roof. The native men dived for their bows and arrows, but were immediately pounced on by Darris and the police. With pistols drawn, Bill and I frantically tried to cover each other and Darris. It was difficult to tell carriers from the natives we were trying to capture.

My torch caught the glint of a knife held by a native standing near Darris. Bill saw the knife in the same instant and yelled as he lunged for it. Darris whirled on the man with his revolver as the knife fell to the floor. A stocky policeman quickly seated the man with another prisoner. Women and children still screamed and, with Nogoi's assistance, Darris tried to calm them: the problem was to convince these primitive people we were not going to kill and eat them.

Three prisoners were now seated on the floor, closely guarded by police. One man screamed at us in his native tongue, and Nogoi quickly interpreted: 'The rest of our tribe at Mogulubi are waiting for you. They will kill and eat you. You will regret this.'

The man, who had never before seen a rifle, refused to be silenced by the threats of a policeman. We took the three men outside, where they were identified by the witness as the three who had raided Masamo a few weeks earlier. Although instructed to stay in the shadows, the witness came too close when identifying the prisoners, and was seen by one of them. The prisoner shouted one word, 'Asa.' In Biami this means, 'Your day will come.'

We kept two policemen with us to guard the prisoners and sent the remaining four into the bush to bring up the rest of the carriers and our supplies. While they were gone we began to question the prisoners and discovered there had been four men sleeping in the house when we surrounded it. One had managed to escape in the confusion.

We were now worried. The policemen had been gone half an hour, and there was a distinct possibility that the man who had escaped might bring the rest of the Mogulubi villagers to attack us. Although we had approximately forty carriers, they could do little against an arrow attack by several hundred tribesmen. We had only our revolvers and two policemen armed with rifles. The five of us sat with our backs together, a few yards from the front of the hut. The prisoners were made to lie on the ground in front of the policemen, and the carriers huddled together in a group at the side of the hut. Each time the breeze stirred the foliage, or a bird or insect made a noise, our fears that we were being silently surrounded by the Mogulubis increased, but the policemen finally returned with the rest of the patrol, and we realised our imaginations had been working overtime.

It was now 4.30. We had just over an hour to reach the main village of Mogulubi before daybreak. Like the men we had just captured in the garden house, the villagers at Mogulubi would not be expecting us until after daylight. Our only chance was to reach Mogulubi and surround the large communal house before dawn. We set off at a swift but silent pace towards Mogulubi,

our three prisoners roped together at the wrists and carefully guarded near the end of the patrol.

The slate-gray light of early morning filtered through the trees, barely lighting the trail. A thick fog hugged the jungle floor. Darris paused and held up his hand for silence.

'We're getting close now,' he whispered. 'The main longhouse is just over that hill.'

We were soon picking our way through large gardens of bananas, taro and yams. Guns drawn, everyone tense. A crashing noise in the bush at the side of the trail and we whirled, at any moment expecting natives to leap from the bushes. Instead, Darris's dog, Esky, came wandering out wagging his tail.

'One more trick like that, Esky, and you'll end up with a bullet between your eyes,' snapped Darris in a hoarse whisper. 'I thought I told you to stay at the post. I'll deal with you later.' And to the rest of us, a whispered command, 'Let's get up that hill.'

On we went. Soon we were on the edge of another clearing. In front of us stood a longhouse, and off to the right a small burial platform on which lay a skeleton. A skull hung from a corner eave of the hut. Darris took four police and made his way down the side of the house towards the front. Bill led the remaining two police, Nogoi and myself across the rear of the hut to move in from the other side. As we approached the burial platform, I moved in close to take pictures.

The same thoughts that had plagued my mind a few hours earlier had now returned: a bone-tipped arrow could hit any one of us at any moment. I sighed with relief as I heard Darris yell, 'It's all right. Come on up. There's only an old man and a young boy here.'

When we reached the front of the house, Darris began questioning the old man with the aid of Nogoi. 'Where are the rest of your people?' he asked.

'They have gone into the bush to hunt,' said the old man. 'My son and I are willing to go with you. Take us and leave our people alone.'

64

. . . off to the right a small burial platform . . . We were later to learn that these were the bones of the old man's elder son, who was killed by the serpent

The same thoughts . . . returned. A bone-
tipped arrow could hit any one of us at
any moment 65

Darris looked puzzled. 'I wonder what they've done,' he said to Bill. 'I find it hard to believe the other villagers are out in the bush hunting when they obviously knew we were coming. There's something fishy going on.'

Darris ordered Nogoi to find the witness from Masamo. The man had refused to return to his village without a police escort. He soon appeared and Darris asked him if either the old man, or his son, had been involved in the raid on his village. He said no, and was sent back outside.

'One thing's certain,' said Darris, 'we're not hanging around this house any longer. If it is an ambush, we're far too vulnerable here, with all that bush so close to the house. Anyway, this isn't one of their main houses. It's just an extra large garden house. That's why the fortifications are so poor. Unless my memory fails me, there's an old abandoned garden house just over the hill. It's high, and will provide a good vantage point. We'll try to make it there, and hole up until we can find out what this is all about.'

For about fifteen minutes we crept through eight-feet kunai grass and old gardens that were littered with rotten logs and abandoned pig barricades. There was a shout from one of the police boys a few yards behind, and we raced back through the grass to see what had happened. He was crouched on one knee, rifle in a firing position. He claimed he had caught a glimpse of two natives, armed with bow and arrows, creeping up behind him. They fled when he turned on them with his rifle. His rifle, like those carried by the other police boys, was not loaded.

The police are not allowed to load their weapons until instructed to do so by the patrol officer. This, of course, prevents undue panic and shooting incidents. Thank God our pistols were loaded and, at times, cocked.

We moved on, even more cautiously than before. As we drew near the foot of the hill, a young boy appeared from the scrub, waving and smiling. It was obvious he was scared, for he jumped

. . . the capture

every time we moved. Nogoi asked him where his people were and, still smiling, he said, 'I will show you. I will take you to them.'

'Sure you will . . . like hell!' said Darris. 'You'll lead us right into an ambush, that's what you'll do.' He told Nogoi to grab the boy and take him with us to the garden house. Perhaps he would answer a few questions there.

After climbing a steep hill we came to a ridge. A path led down to a small hut perched on stilts overlooking the dense forest. Darris was right. It was a good vantage point. We took Nogoi and the prisoners up the ladder and inside. A police guard was posted on all sides of the house, and the carriers told to gather under and around the house as they arrived. The cook boy used a cube of dry fuel to boil canteen water for coffee. We sat on the floor of the hut and lit a cigarette.

'Now,' Darris instructed Nogoi, 'ask the old man and his son why they think the Government wants to take them away.'

As the old man was questioned the following story unfolded: 'It was just over two months ago when my oldest son died. A serpent bit him. His bones lay at the house where we waited for you. I talked with great sorrow to my youngest son who is now at my side. After much thinking, we knew that someone from the village of Adumari had put a spell on us and caused my son's death. If I were younger, I would have gone alone to Adumari, but I am old and weak. My son was not yet a man and too small to handle such things by himself. About three weeks ago, I went with my son to Adumari. We hid in the garden and waited. Two days passed. On the third day a man walked alone through the garden. I crept up behind and grabbed him with both arms. My son hacked at his face and head with a stone axe. My son is now a man.'

Darris ordered two police boys to guide the prisoners, who now numbered six—the three men caught in the first house who had raided Masamo Village, the old man and his son, and the young boy we suspected of trying to lead us into an ambush.

We walked outside and sat on a patrol box while we drank hot coffee and ate soggy biscuits. There was complete silence among the carriers and police, everyone intently watching the bushline for signs of movement.

Darris broke the silence. 'I know there's something funny going on here, but I can't endanger the whole patrol just to find out what it is. After all, it may be nothing. It's hard to tell with these people. You never know exactly what they're up to. We'll take the old man and his boy back to Nomad and charge them, and send the kid we just grabbed back to his people with a message from the Government.'

Nogoi brought the boy from the house and sat him down in front of us. Darris reached into a patrol box behind him and pulled out a hatchet. With Nogoi interpreting, he told the boy, 'Take this hatchet to your people and tell them it is a gift from the Government. The Government does not wish to harm your people. We are your friends. We want to help you. We will give you white man's medicine for your sick, and axes and knives to make your work easier. But you must stop killing and eating each other. If you continue your killing, we will have to take you away as we have the old man and his son. We will return to your village in a few months' time and, if you have obeyed our law, we will do you no harm. You have had visits from the Government before, and the Government has been friendly in the past. Trust us, we are your friends.'

The boy was then told to return to his people, and we prepared to move out.

'I want to get out of here before there's any trouble,' said Darris. 'The boy just might be able to get our message across, but if there's bloodshed, it'll take months to repair the damage. Besides, we've still got a good eight to nine-hour walk ahead to get to base camp.'

Right: 'You'll lead us right into an ambush, that's what you'll do'

'I crept up behind and grabbed him with both arms . . .'

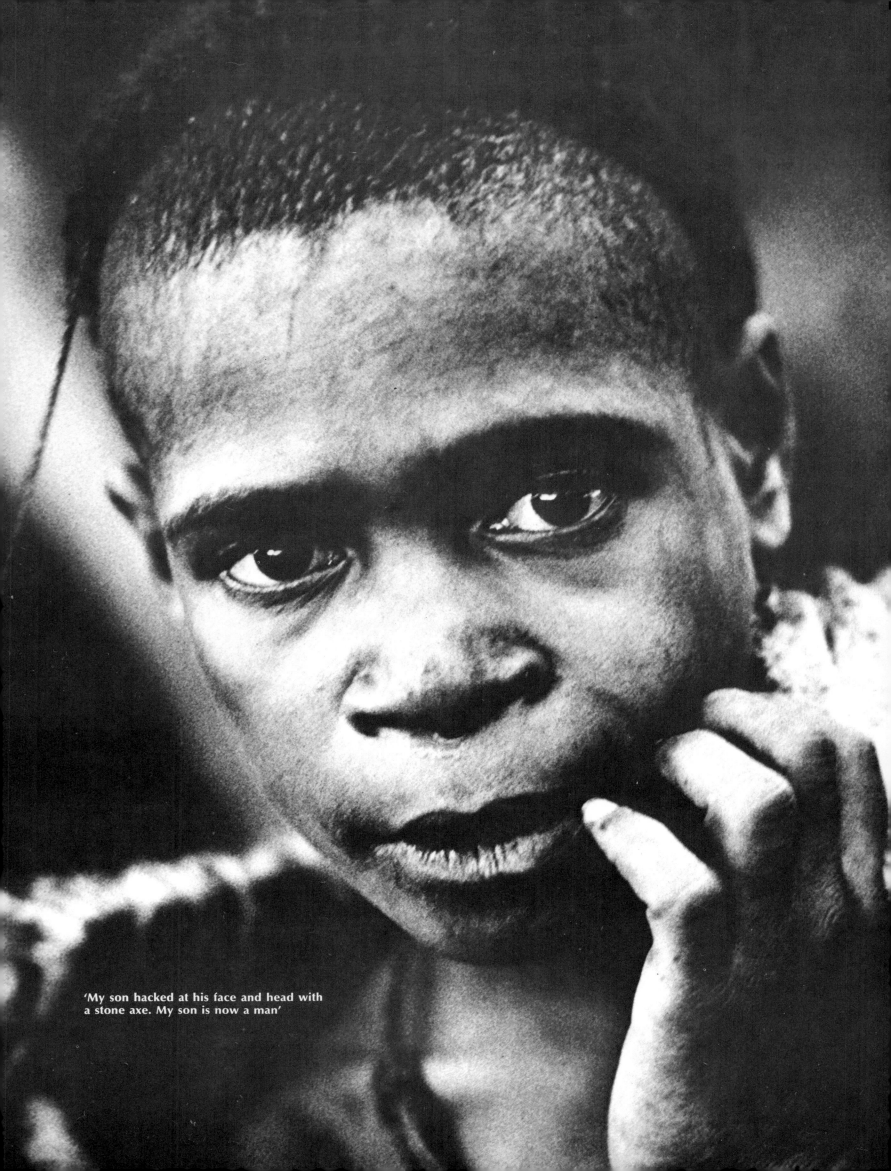

'My son hacked at his face and head with a stone axe. My son is now a man'

No one was particularly happy about the walk that lay ahead. We had already been on our feet seven hours.

The first couple of hours went fairly quickly, then each hour seemed to drag more slowly. I began to ache from head to toe, and found myself falling as much as walking. Before leaving Masamo, I had soaked my boots in dieseline, and rubbed them with salt to ward off the leeches. By now the dieseline had begun to wear off, and the slimy leeches worked their way up my pants legs.

I reached in my pocket for the diesoline and noticed blood on the front of my shirt. I unbuttoned it and looked inside, but could see nothing. Then I ran my hands over my face and down my neck, and there it was, a huge leech dangling from my throat. I pulled it off in disgust and continued to soak my boots and shirt with repelent.

Soon we were climbing, and a rain-soaked ridge loomed high above us. Muddy, wet leaves, bigger than a large hand, slapped at my face as I struggled for a foothold. It was almost 12.30 and we still had at least three hours to go. My feet and legs felt numb as I tripped and stumbled over stones and tree roots.

A shout from Darris snapped me out of the trance: 'Get on the seat of your pants and watch out for sharp stones. Just don't try to walk.' We were sliding down a muddy ridge, almost vertical in places, and I grabbed at a passing tree and was jerked around, face down in the mud.

A few minutes later we were at the base of the ridge, on the banks of a raging river. With gunbelts strung across our shoulders we waded through the almost icy waters, reached the other side and collapsed exhausted on the gravel.

After a short rest, we saw a large green snake slither across a boulder about fifty yards down river. Nogoi sat near us with a bundle of arrows and a bow, confiscated from one of the prisoners. Darris grabbed the bow and an arrow and aimed at the snake. I laughed to myself, and Bill said, 'You must be joking, Darris. You couldn't hit the broad side of a barn with one of those things.'

Darris drew back the bowstring and fired. The arrow found its mark about eight inches behind the snake's head. While Bill and I looked on, mouths gaping, Darris casually handed the bow back to Nogoi, lay back across the patrol box and stretched as he sighed, 'You guys just don't know a marksman when you see one.'

Bill chuckled, 'Sure Darris, sure. Just consider yourself lucky Jim and I are too bloody tired to throw you in the river. You couldn't do that again with a .45, much less a bow and arrow.'

'Too bad you'll never know,' said Darris, and we all laughed as Nogoi came back with the snake still on the end of the arrow.

The police had just brought the prisoners across the river, and the last of the carriers were now catching up. It's bad enough moving through this lousy jungle with both hands free, I thought to myself, but I sure wouldn't like to try it with one hand tied by a rope to four other people. The prisoners, however, didn't look any the worse for wear.

We had rested for almost twenty minutes and it was time to move on. Only the thought of a full day's rest at Obami, still about a two-hour walk away encouraged me to go on.

About an hour and a half later, just as I thought my numbed feet couldn't possibly take another step, the carriers suddenly broke out with wild whooping calls and began running past me. I had fallen behind, and Darris and Bill were well out of sight. A few moments later I stumbled out of the bush on to a clear track about eight feet wide. With a bit of smoothing, I thought to myself, you could drive a Landrover on this. Maybe if I just sat alongside the road, a Government Landrover, or perhaps even a taxi or bus, would come by and pick me up.

Previous page: There was complete silence among the carriers and police, everyone intently watching the bushline for signs of movement

. . . the slimy leeches worked their way
up our legs

. . . tripped and stumbled over stones
and tree roots

. . . wet leaves, bigger than a large hand

'You must be joking, Darris. You couldn't hit the broad side of a barn . . .'

With gun belts slung across our shoulders we waded through the almost icy waters

76

Only the thought of a full day's rest . . .
encouraged me to go on

'Obami stop long op'

77

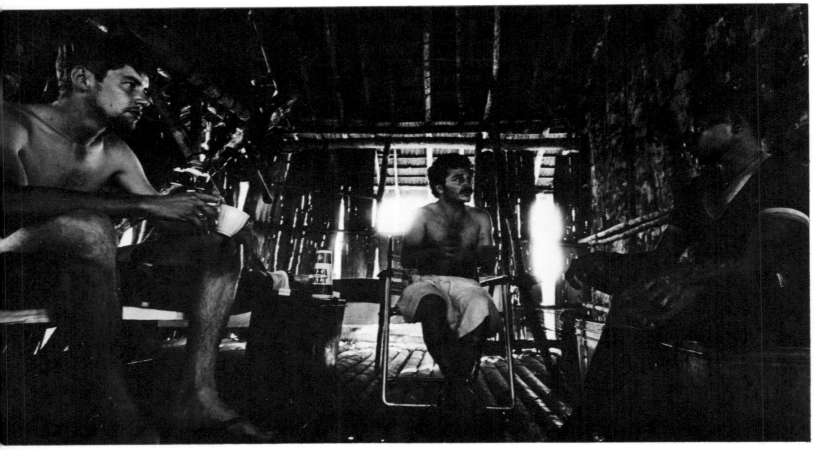

The whooping of the carriers brought me back to reality. I picked up the two poles I had been using as crutches for the last hour and hobbled on down the track. Carriers were still racing past me, carrying the patrol boxes, shouting and singing as they went. I knew we must be close.

Twenty minutes later I came to a small bridge, and at the top of the hill on the other side stood a group of thatch-roofed huts. By now I was on my own except for one police boy who had stayed back to help me. He pointed to the huts and said, 'Obami stop long op.'

I staggered up the steps to the hut in time to see both Bill and Darris struggling to get their boots off. They had collapsed into the faithful old aluminium folding chairs.

Darris looked up, smiled and asked, 'What took you so long, mate?'

'Oh, nothing,' I said, 'Just stopped to pick daises along the way. Nothing like a fourteen-hour stroll to make a man appreciate Nature.'

For the remainder of the afternoon we lay in our bedsleeves and nursed blisters. We had walked between fifteen and twenty miles, but it seemed like hundreds.

The crackling of the radio awakened me. Darris was bringing Alan up to date on the day's events. 'Bill will bring the five prisoners back the day after tomorrow, Alan. We'll rest up here tomorrow, to give our legs a chance to sober up.'

'Roger, Darris. When are you and Jim leaving for the Rentoul River?'

'On Sunday, as far as I know now, same time Bill leaves for Nomad.'

'Roger, Dee. Any idea when you'll get back to base camp? Over.'

'Yes, Alan, we should be gone about a week, providing we don't have any trouble, or get lost. Over.'

'I'll try to meet you at base camp on about the 13th then. Bill will be able to hold the fort here, and I want to do a patrol into the Gubusi area. Okay?'

'Right, Alan. Look forward to seeing you on the 13th. I'll call you again on Monday to make sure Bill got back all right. Cheers, and out for now.'

As Darris signed off, Nogoi appeared at the door of the hut and motioned us outside. I hobbled to the door with Darris and looked out over nearly two hundred carriers and tribesmen from nearby Obami village. There were huge piles of bananas and kaukau stacked high at the steps of the hut. Darris brought out the trade goods and told Nogoi to buy food for the carriers.

As we headed back for our beds, Nogoi called us again. It seemed a number of the carriers wanted to be paid off and go back to Nomad. They hadn't liked the day's walk any more than we had, and didn't particularly like the idea of going into unknown regions along the Rentoul River.

'There's nothing wrong with them that a good day's rest won't cure,' said Darris. 'We'll stall them until we're ready to leave. Any that still want to return to Nomad then, I'll pay off.'

We again dined on fresh pig that night and retired, exhausted about seven.

Next day was spent resting and cleaning our guns and equipment. And that afternoon Darris sent Nogoi with a message that any carriers who still wished to return to Nomad could collect their pay. Only six did, and they were paid off with knives and calico. That night, after a card game and a hot shower, we once more retired early. Although Darris had only a four-hour walk planned for the following day, Bill's return to Nomad with the prisoners would take him eight or nine hours by the main trail. We had come the long way, via Mogulubi.

With any luck, in the next few days, we would be visiting villages that no white men had ever seen.

Top left: Questioning the prisoners again at base camp before their return to Nomad

Left: Darris briefs Nogoi at base camp on tomorrow's work

THE UNDISCOVERED

Bill left for Nomad about five o'clock in the morning, and by eight Darris and I had our jungle boots laced up and soaked in dieseline. The six or seven-hour walk that lay ahead would take us to the village of Sedado, and didn't look so bad after our two-day rest. As we walked, I noticed Nogoi stumbling along in front of us. I kept watching him, knowing something was wrong but unable to put my finger on it. I touched Darris on the shoulder and asked if he had noticed anything strange about Nogoi.

'Yeah,' he said. 'He seems awfully bloody clumsy this morning. Tripping over everything in sight . . . Hey, wait a minute, he's got boots on! Nogoi, hold up for a minute.'

We caught up with him and I noticed something else was wrong. He not only had boots on, but had them on the wrong feet. We stopped for a cigarette and tackled Nogoi about his newly-acquired footwear. Seems he had managed to swindle one of the police boys out of an old worn-out pair. He didn't, however, realise it made a difference which boot went on which foot. As we moved on, Darris remarked, 'I'll give him about three hours in those boots. What's the bet he has them off before we get to Ubulufi?'

We arrived at Ubulufi about 11.30. The main longhouse was about 250ft long and reputed to be the biggest in the Biami area. Three sets of bones, bleached white by the sun, lay on a burial platform at the corner of the house. We gathered near the drop-log front door of the longhouse, and several villagers appeared and began shaking hands and snapping their fingers in traditional greeting.

'The skeletons on the burial platform,' explained Darris, 'were tribesmen killed in a raid by the village of Obami, near base camp. Several of the tribesmen were locked up over it and they have been more or less behaving themselves since.'

I noticed a peculiar-looking birdcage structure situated near the burial platform, and Darris and I walked over to examine it. As we approached we saw several skulls inside. It was a burial platform for a chief or an important man of the tribe and was shaped like a small altar, about six or eight feet off the ground, sheltered by a bark roof.

The weather closed in and a light rain began to fall as we made our way towards Sedado. We arrived about two that afternoon, thoroughly soaked. Camp was pitched rather hurriedly, and at eight that evening, as we prepared to

Left: 'Yeah,' he said. 'He seems awfully bloody clumsy this morning'

Overleaf: The main longhouse at Ubulufi —over 250 feet long

retire, the rain became heavier and more menacing. Darris was worried the continual downpour might flood the Alagumia River. We would come to it about half an hour out the following morning, and if it had become too swollen to cross we would have to camp on the banks for possibly two days. At least we had plenty of food, I thought to myself. And the villagers had brought down more than 1000 pounds of bananas shortly after we arrived. We had purchased the lot as food for the carriers.

I lay thinking about the day's events and fascinated by the sound of the rain pelting on the roof of the tent. A bird of paradise called to its mate across the trees. Then every bird of paradise in the area joined in, and the cicadas immediately tried to drown them out. Owls hooted their annoyance and the whole jungle became a riot of noise.

I couldn't sleep, so I unpacked the tape recorder. It was two hours later when I slipped back under my mosquito net. Darris was still snoring, oblivious to the commotion around him.

The rain was still heavy next morning, and the leeches were out in their thousands. The ground was slippery and we found ourselves constantly falling over wet, mossy logs, and wading knee-deep in slimy mud. We were travelling across the grain of the ridges, grasping for tree-roots as our feet slid from under us, climbing on all fours to the top of a rise and then skidding down into a valley again, there to face a raging stream that sliced through the gorge. The Alagumia took us almost half an hour to cross. We had to walk downstream several hundred yards before finding a suitably shallow spot.

With water up to our waists, we poled our way across, step by treacherous step.

By the time we reached Abodo, anything which wasn't wet from river crossings was soaked with sweat or bloody from leech bites. We made camp at Abodo and Darris jumped in first for a hot shower. Then it was my turn, and the hot water felt so good I got carried away and next thing I knew I was standing, fully-soaped, in the cool damp air with not a drop left in the shower bucket.

I hollered for the cookie, but unfortunately he'd used the last of the water to boil spuds, so I stood there and almost froze for forty minutes while two of the carriers ran down to the river to fetch more water for the cookie to heat. At last I flopped into my bedsleeve for a rest.

A few minutes later the cookie pulled up a patrol box between the bedsleeves and served coffee along with one of the tastiest treats of the patrol, pan-fried bread with a can of smoked oysters. As he served, he said, 'Me sorry water finish, Taba.' I told him oyster bread made up for anything.

Soon after, a group of natives entered the camp with the usual bundles of bananas and taro. Darris sent Nogoi out to bargain with them, then he turned to me and said. 'You know, Jim, these people have really come along fast. In May, only five months ago, Alan and myself visited Abodo for the first time. Only four men stayed to meet us, but after we explained we had come in peace and wished them no harm, they invited us in to the longhouse where we presented them with an axe and some matches, calico and salt, and gave them a villlage book. At that time there was a human thigh lying in the smoke basket over the fire. We discreetly explained that they must stop killing and eating each other, and to date they have—or they're being awfully sneaky about it if they haven't. Frankly, I suspect the latter, yet the two or three patrols that have visited here since our first contact have been without incident. I guess we'll just have to wait and see.'

Top left: We had to walk downstream several hundred yards before finding a suitably shallow spot

Left: Three sets of bones . . . lay on a burial platform at the corner of the house 85

About five that evening the cookie walked in from the bush with a large fowl in one hand and a shotgun in the other. He'd been out hunting for almost two hours and Darris had been about to send a police boy out to look for him. That night's meal consisted of the fowl cooked in a pressure cooker, fresh jungle greens and fried taro and yams, followed by canned chocolate cake and cream for dessert.

Darris lay back after the meal, lit a cigarette, and said, 'I think you'd better run out of shower water every night from now on. It's very seldom cookie feeds me like this.'

That night the mosquitos were un-usually thick, so we crawled under our nets very early and read by the light of the kersosene lamp until we fell asleep.

We were up and walking by six the next morning. We passed through Masama about 8.30, and the smell of death was heavy in the air. There was a corpse on a burial platform outside the longhouse that must have been four or five weeks old. Underneath the fighting platform hung several skulls, taken in raids. We made enquiries about the villages on the Rentoul River that Darris had spotted from the air, but no one came forward with information.

We arrived at Samodoro about ten, and again tried to get information about the villages, but as soon as we started asking questions, the tribesmen ran into the bush and hid. For some unknown reason they not only refused to give us directions, but denied the existence of any such villages on the Rentoul. We boiled the billy and had coffee before leaving.

En route to the next village we stopped for almost an hour to play photographic hide and seek with the bird of paradise. Although usually rare and elusive, they were as thick as sparrows in this particular area, chattering and squeaking as they hopped from limb to limb in tree-tops high above us. Their bright red and yellow tails

Right: . . . the smell of death was heavy in the air
Far right: We were up and walking by six the next morning

86

bobbed frantically as they performed their strange and fascinating dance.

We arrived at the village of Dimarifi about 1.30 that afternoon, but it was deserted, and we assumed the people were out hunting or working in the gardens.

After a brief rest we moved on to Kogoyabi, about a forty-five-minute walk away. We set up camp, and bunked inside a hut built by a previous patrol officer. We'd walked more than ten miles that day, but fortunately the trek had been broken with pauses at several villages. The Kogoyabi longhouse was only one hundred yards from our campsite and at the rear of the fighting platform were two decaying bodies. At the time we camped we were upwind of them, but just as the evening meal was placed before us the wind changed, and neither Darris nor I was able to eat much that night.

Next morning a number of villagers came to us with infected cuts and sores. The medical orderly treated them. As we broke camp, one of the police boys reported that three carriers from Sedado had deserted during the night, taking with them a patrol box containing axes and knives.

The carriers were afraid to enter an area where not even the Government had previously been. Several other carriers asked to be paid off and allowed to go back to base camp, but abandoned the idea when reminded they would have to return alone.

We finally set off about nine, the walking rougher than on the previous day because we had changed direction and once more had to climb up and down ridges instead of travel along them. The ridges ran north-south and we were following narrow, barely-visible trails, working around in an easterly direction towards the Rentoul.

We had no idea where the next village lay or when we would find it. About 11.30, as we worked our way

Top left: Underneath the fighting platform hung several skulls taken in raids

Left: The rare and elusive bird of paradise . . .

down the side of a slippery ridge, we saw a garden house in the valley below, and glimpsed the backsides of three tribesmen as they fled into the bush. We approached the house slowly, Nogoi hollering, 'Friend . . . Brother . . . We come in peace!'

The house was deserted, the inside walls lined with hundreds of bone-tipped arrows. Several fighting clubs lay on the earthen floor in one corner. We left and followed the trail deeper into the valley.

'The main longhouse must be fairly close,' said Darris. About twenty minutes later we saw the house on a ridge to the left. Again, as we approached, a number of villagers ran into the bush. Five men with curly black beards stood tall and erect in front of the house. 'They must be the village fight leaders,' explained Darris.

We approached slowly, Nogoi yelling as before, 'Friend . . . Brothers . . . We come in peace!' Although they smiled as we drew near, they were obviously afraid.

'Don't make any quick movements,' warned Darris. 'Don't even reach for a cigarette, or they'll be off into the bush before you can get it to your mouth.'

We paused about ten feet away and sat on a log. Now, with Nogoi chatting to them in their own language about the Government, Darris and I slowly lit a smoke. Our revolver holsters had been unsnapped since we had approached the first garden house, but the atmosphere soon relaxed and the tribesmen squatted on the ground before us, chattering and gesturing excitely. We gave each a cigarette, matches and a razorblade and Darris began to question them. One had seen a European three or four years before, and Darris assumed this had been Patrol Officer Hode, who had circled through the area a little further north in 1963.

'That was in the old village,' said the man. 'You are the first white men to visit this village.'

. . . the inside walls were lined with hundreds of bone-tipped arrows. Several fighting clubs lay on the floor . . .

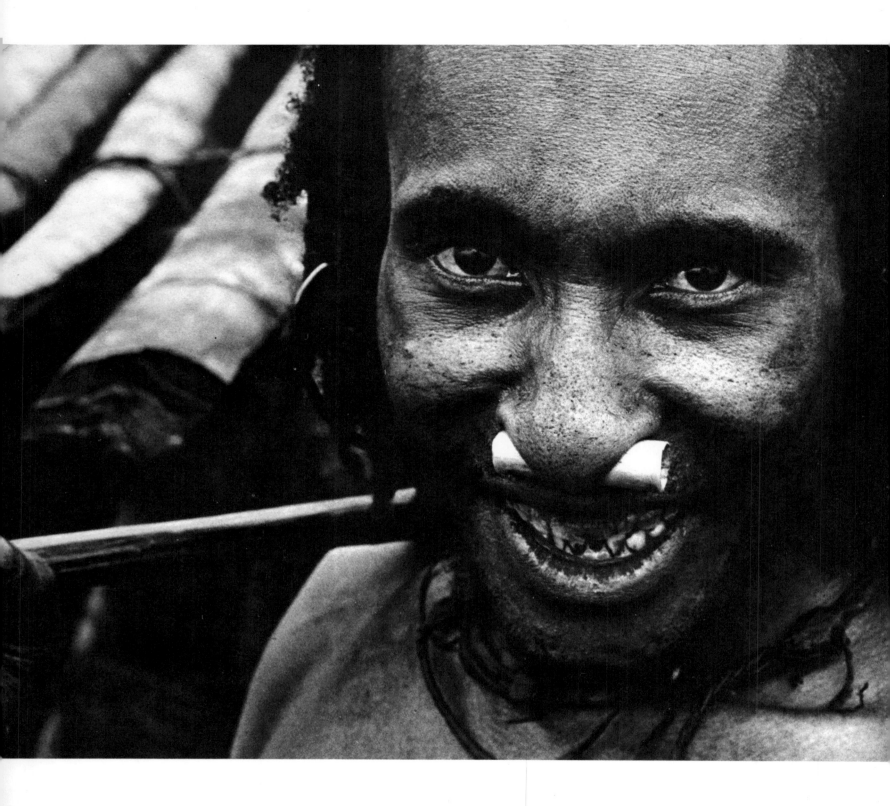

The four younger men gazed at us intently, obviously amazed by our white skins and peculiar dress. We were the first white men they had seen. Eventually they took us into their longhouse. Again, the walls were lined with bone-tipped arrows, and at every few feet a black palm bow. A number of kunda drums hung by a piece of bark near the centre of the hut. In the main foyer of the house were the ashes of six burned-out fires and a smoking basket hanging above each.

At the rear, a short ladder descended about eight feet to another level of the house. A corridor running through this section of the house led to a fighting platform at the rear. On each side of the corridor were small cubicles, each with

The atmosphere seemed relaxed

Tribesmen squatted on the ground before us . . .

its own bark mat, where the women slept. The men slept around the fires in the main part of the house, and counting the bark beds of the women, and multiplying them by four, Darris estimated the village population at almost two hundred.

We left and made camp nearby in the hope that more villagers would venture in from the bush during that afternoon. Darris instructed Nogoi to ask the fighting men for any bananas or kaukau they could spare. In return we would give them razorblades, matches, calico, and salt, with which they were already familiar. Salt had been traded in from other villages near base camp, and we later discovered the village also possessed a steel axe and two steel knives. (This is not particularly unusual.) Seashell necklaces are one of the main items used in the area to purchase a bride. Practically every man over twelve years of age has at least one or two necklaces or headbands made from seashells— yet the Gulf of Papua, where the necklaces are made, is at least 700 miles away. The trading routes are more complex than one would imagine.

Later that afternoon seven or eight more village men appeared, but no women or children. They brought in the bananas and the kaukau, and a pig, for which we traded an axe. We also brought a number of stone clubs and axes and after the bartering had finished, Darris gave them another talk about the Government. We were then able to determine the village name—Guamari.

That night, about six, several hundred feet of rope were strung up in a circle around the camp, and Nogoi was told to inform the villagers they were not allowed inside the rope after dark. An extra police guard was posted as an added precaution.

'There's always the chance of a misunderstanding,' explained Darris. 'In that case the villagers will often grab their bows and prepare for battle before things can be sorted out. Their curiosity about the white man's strange possessions can also cause problems, and if there's a problem during the night it's much easier to cope with knowing where they are or, to be more exact, knowing where they're not.'

We ate fresh pork again that night and retired early, our revolvers beside us on the bedsleeve. The night passed without incident and we broke camp about eight next morning. Two hours later we arrived at the village of Giwagafi, and were greeted by several men, but again saw no women or children. They already knew of our presence in the area and were expecting us, which made the situation far less tense. A runner had obviously been sent from Guamari the night before. We stayed only long enough to tell them about the Government, and to give them a village book.

We moved on and arrived at a third previously unvisited village about noon and made camp. There was no one in sight when we arrived, but soon after we had made camp a number of men and women came with food they had gathered from their gardens in anticipation of our visit. When we talked with the villagers that afternoon we discovered that three or four of the men had been to Obami when it was first established and had worked at setting up the base camp. Most of the men and virtually all of the women and children had never seen a white man.

With three new villages on the map, Darris sat up late that night writing reports. Next morning we packed and left for Samodoro. We had been out six days now and supplies were running low. We stopped at Samodoro only long enough to make an entry in the village book, and then trudged on to Obami.

Previous page, left: 'You are the first white men to visit this village'
Previous page, right: . . . amazed by our white skins and peculiar dress
Right: Seashell necklaces are one of the main items used in the area to purchase a bride

95

BASE CAMP

On arrival at Base Camp we discovered things had been far from quiet during our absence. One of the police boys reported that the day before about forty tribesmen from nearby Sedado had come to demand axes and knives for work contracts they had not yet completed. They had threatened to burn their village book and take up arms if they were not immediately paid. The police constable had tried to stall them until our return but had finally given up, fearing retaliation.

'Looks like I'll have to smarten up those Sedados a bit,' said Darris. 'Remember the three carriers who deserted with a box of axes and knives? They were also from Sedado. As soon as Alan arrives we'll go down and straighten them out.'

That afternoon we got through to Bill on the radio at Nomad. Things weren't exactly quiet there, either. The Mogulubi man and his son we had arrested the week before had escaped. Whether they'd make it back to Mogulubi or finish up as food for some village on the way, was anybody's guess.

Also, the villagers of Walibi, about halfway between Base Camp and Nomad, had threatened a policeman and two carriers who were returning from Base Camp after delivering supplies. They told the constable, 'The Government is not welcome here, and will not be allowed to use the track through our village. The next Government patrol that comes near our village, we will kill and eat.'

Darris signed off after being told Alan was on his way and should be arriving tomorrow, but just as he was about to switch off a faint voice came through.

'Portable Portable Obami.'

Darris grabbed the mike again! 'Obami Portable, Obami Portable, reading you Alan, come in please.'

'Been trying to reach you or Bill for the last hour, Darris. I'm somewhere in the Wamoso area, and a bit lost I'm afraid. Do you read me? Over.'

'Right, Alan. You're fading, but read you as being lost. Over.'

'Roger, Darris. I should be within five or six miles from Obami. Can you fire shots tonight and in the morning? I'll be following a compass course. Over.'

'Roger, Alan. Will fire shots tonight, and every hour from seven in the morning until you get here.'

Alan's voice came back very faintly, 'Roger, over and out.'

'Funny about these portable radios,' said Darris, as he switched it off, 'sometimes you can hear them for hundreds of miles, and other times you're lucky to reach someone a couple of miles away. Oh well, at least when we have trouble around here, it all comes at once. When Alan gets here tomorrow, we'll take a day trip down to Sedado, fix up the trouble there, then spend another night

Carriers line up, to be paid by the Patrol Officer, in front of thatch-roofed huts that form the base camp at Obami

here before returning to Nomad via Walibi.

'I wouldn't mind going back to Mogulubi to get the old man and his son, but it's too far out of our way and there's no guarantee they'll be there anyway. I'll give them a month or two and let them think they're safe and free, then we'll go back and grab them when they least expect it.'

We'd been moving fairly steadily for the past few days and, with all the rain, most of our gear had stayed wet, but it was now a bright sunny day, and cookie spread our moulding clothes and canvas gear out to dry. Our crusted boots were scrubbed and placed on stakes outside the hut to dry.

An hour or so later we heard a small commotion outside the hut. Seven or eight tribesmen who had tagged along with the patrol from the Southern Rentoul area were clustered near our staked boots, jabbering excitedly. The noise had even aroused Nogoi's curiosity, and he appeared from the police hut in long striped pyjamas and a singlet.

Darris called him over, muttering something under his breath about 'black boots and striped pyjamas' as he approached.

'What's all the noise about, Nogoi?' asked Darris.

Nogoi turned and spoke to the tribesmen and, after another five minutes of chattering, explained that the tribesmen were confused. They wondered how we had taken off our feet, and for what reason we had placed them upside down on sticks. Nogoi attempted to explain that what they saw on the stakes were only boots, but they still stared and chattered in amazement.

As we walked back up the steps of the hut, Darris yelled, 'By the way, Nogoi, what happened to your boots?'

Top left: '. . . black boots and striped pyjamas . . .'

Left: '. . . a bit confused'

Nogoi looked up and smiled, 'Me no savvy master. What boots?'

I spent the rest of the afternoon cleaning photographic and recording equipment which, it seemed, had began to sprout mushrooms in the wet and humid conditions.

One of the police boys fired three shots every hour next morning, and Alan finally appeared about eleven.

After resting for a couple of hours and having lunch, we set off for Sedado with an escort of eight police boys. Near the village we met four tribesmen, who told us that the three carriers who had deserted the patrol had not yet returned to the village. Also, one of the village elders had died and the village was now in mourning.

'This puts a different complexion on things,' said Darris as we proceeded 'We can't do anything about the carriers until they return, and while they're so upset I don't fancy tackling them about demanding their pay.'

We arrived at the village about thirty minutes later. The body of the village elder had been placed inside the main longhouse, and a pungent odour drifted out to where we were standing. Three villagers were sitting on the ladder leading to the longhouse door, axes in hand and menacing looks on their faces. Other villagers were milling around the clearing in front of the house. We approached cautiously and Darris began talking to them through Nogoi.

'The Government shares your sorrow over the death of your leader. We are sorry to intrude at this time, but a group of your villagers a few days ago threatened the policeman in charge at Obami. Also, three of your people who were employed by the Government as carriers deserted the patrol last week, taking with them a number of axes and knives. These three must

Alan finally appeared . . .

Near Sedado we met four tribesmen . . .

be punished, and the axes and knives they stole returned.'

An old man with a long grey beard stepped forward and shook Darris's hand, snapping fingers in traditional greeting as their hands parted. 'My people mourn my brother's death,' he said. 'The three young men from your patrol have not yet returned. If they have stolen from the Government, then I agree they must be punished. A group of our people went to Obami a few days ago to demand their pay because they heard rumours that you were in the south and possibly would not return. We are sorry, and hope the Government will still be our friend.'

Darris told them the Government would overlook the incident at Obami, but that the three carriers must be sent to base camp when they returned. Darris then decided he had made his point and there was no reason to disturb the villagers further with our presence, so we made our way back to base camp.

Left: We approached cautiously . . .

Snapping fingers in traditional greeting

RETURN TO CIVILISATION

It was hot and steamy next morning as our patrol stretched out in a snake-like line towards Walibi. We were on our way home. With any luck we would spend only one more night in the bush, and the following night we'd be having cold beer and ice in our drinks. Again we crossed the grain on many ridges—climb, slide down, climb again—the same monotonous routine, over and over. We passed through three villages on the way, and saw burial platforms bearing two decaying bodies near the track at the first.

It was almost 1.30 as we neared Walibi. Darris told the carriers to follow on a few minutes behind us to avoid unnecessary noise that might warn the villagers of our approach. However, when we arrived at the village a few minutes later it was deserted, except for one small puppy, alone and yapping as we entered the longhouse. Inside, fires were still smouldering, indicating that the villagers had fled only moments before.

The rest of the patrol arrived and we made camp in a rest house built for the Government by the Walibi villagers six or eight months previously. Darris was worried: the Walibi villagers had always been reasonably friendly towards the Government, but it was probably only some trivial matter, such as a patrol carrier walking on, or taking a taro or yams from their garden, that had caused the present hostility. If only we could talk to some of the villagers, the matter could probably be settled in minutes, with an axe or knives given as compensation.

We made camp, and Darris assigned six police boys to keep an all-night guard, while Nogoi called to the villagers who, we suspected, were hiding nearby. He called all afternoon, but with the exception of the occasional rustle in the bush, there was no reply.

About four that afternoon Darris sent two police boys with half a dozen carriers to the village garden to take what food we needed so that the patrol could proceed to Nomad. Next morning, before leaving, we placed matches, razorblades and calico inside the longhouse, as payment for what we had taken.

From the village we descended along a steep hillside to the banks of the Kuma. A large tree that patrols normally used to cross the river had been washed away from the opposite bank, and we were held up for almost two hours while rafts were made to ferry patrol boxes across two at a time.

Finally we gathered on the far bank, climbed the ridge, and looked back on the village of Walibi. The fighting platform was clearly visible and on it stood a number of villagers, waving bows and arrows and shouting. Nogoi

As we neared Walibi, a grim warning was sighted in a tall tree beside the track . . . human bones wedged in the branches about ten feet up

translated, 'We don't want white men here . . . We don't want the Government to use the track through our village . . . The next white men who come to our village we will shoot and eat.'

Who knows what lies in store for the next patrol into the area? More than likely the Walibi villagers will again run away and hide. Only time will tell.

Two and a half hours later we broke out of the jungle on to the end of the Nomad airstrip. In the distance were the thatch-roofed huts and the Australian flag fluttering in the breeze. We were home. Darris and I headed straight for the refrigerator. Bill just grinned as we raced past him with a very brief, 'Hi, how're things?' After a long spell of drinking that beautifully icy beer, we checked the carriers and the gear.

A handful of natives from villages we had visited had decided that they too would work for the Government and had tagged along with the patrol. Now they stood in a small group at the edge of the football field, not knowing what to do with themselves. Darris called them over, found Nogoi, and took them on a tour of the station.

Back to the beer. But this time we also took the villagers. They had never seen ice or water taps, glass windows or lights that turned on by flicking a switch on the wall. One of the interpreters took the hand of a small boy and laid it on the ice inside the freezer compartment of a refrigerator. The look that crossed that boy's face had us in fits of laughter.

Left: The rest of our patrol arrived . . .

Nogoi called the villagers who, we suspected, were hiding nearby

. . . rafts were made to ferry patrol boxes across the Kuma River

Right: They had never seen ice or water taps, glass windows, or lights that turned on by flicking a switch

One of the interpreters took the hand of a small boy and laid it on the ice . . .

For almost a month we had turned our backs on the atomic-age and stepped into a stone-age world that has changed little in the past thousand years. The truth could be seen in the faces of the laughing villagers. There was much they didn't understand. What the white man has grown accustomed to over hundreds of years, these natives would have to adjust to in a matter of months.

Their traditional way of life irretrievably shattered by the rape of progress, many would at first rebel. But, and somewhat sadly I thought, the burial platforms, the longhouses, the fightleaders, the very culture, all these would die as the young men of the villages discovered the white man's way of life. They would move to the patrol stations and towns to work for the Government their fathers had feared and resented.

I left Nomad feeling I had lived for a short space in another world. Now that I am back in civilisation, only my photographs prove to me that this other world exists.

His traditional way of life soon to be shattered by the rape of progress . . .

108

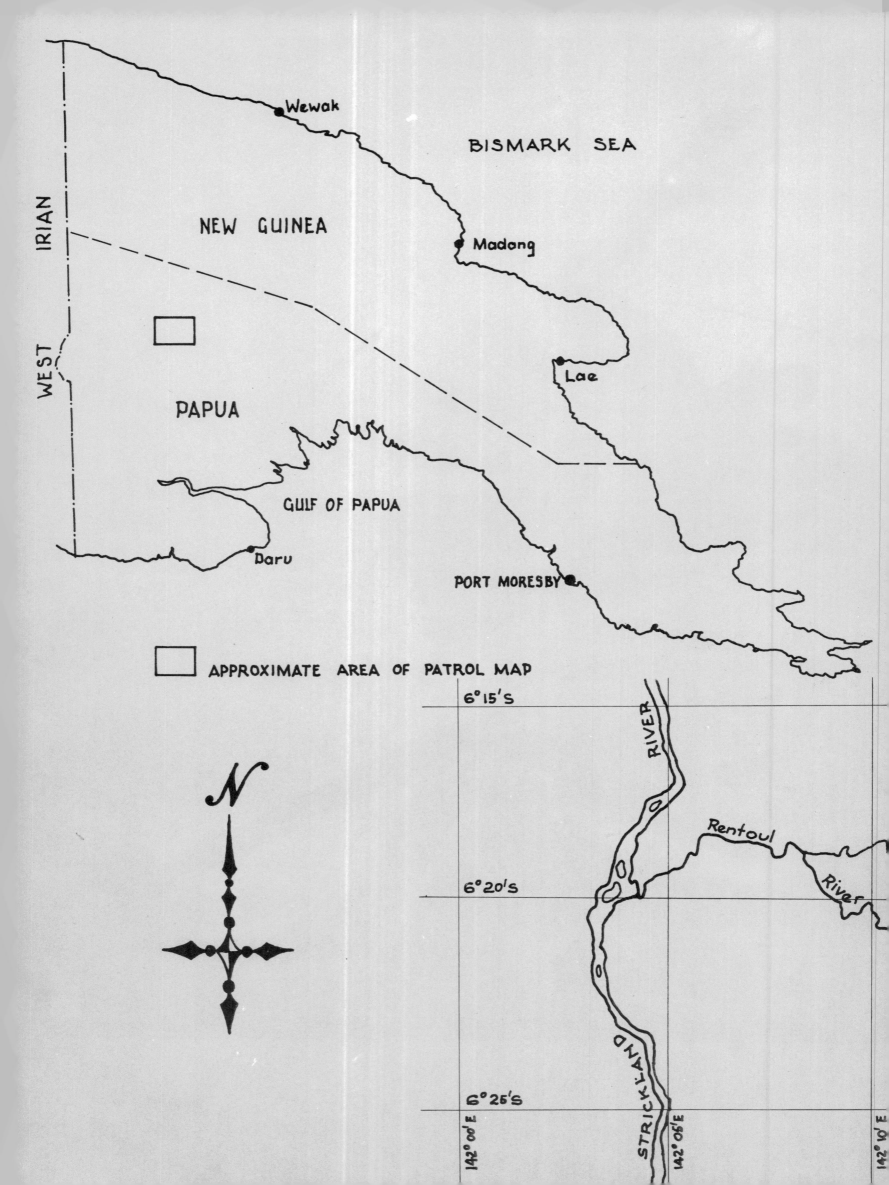

BISMARK SEA

WEST IRIAN

NEW GUINEA

PAPUA

Wewak

Madang

Lae

GULF OF PAPUA

Daru

PORT MORESBY

☐ APPROXIMATE AREA OF PATROL MAP

N

6°15'S

6°20'S

6°25'S

RIVER

Rentoul

River

STRICKLAND

142°00'E

142°05'E

142°10'E

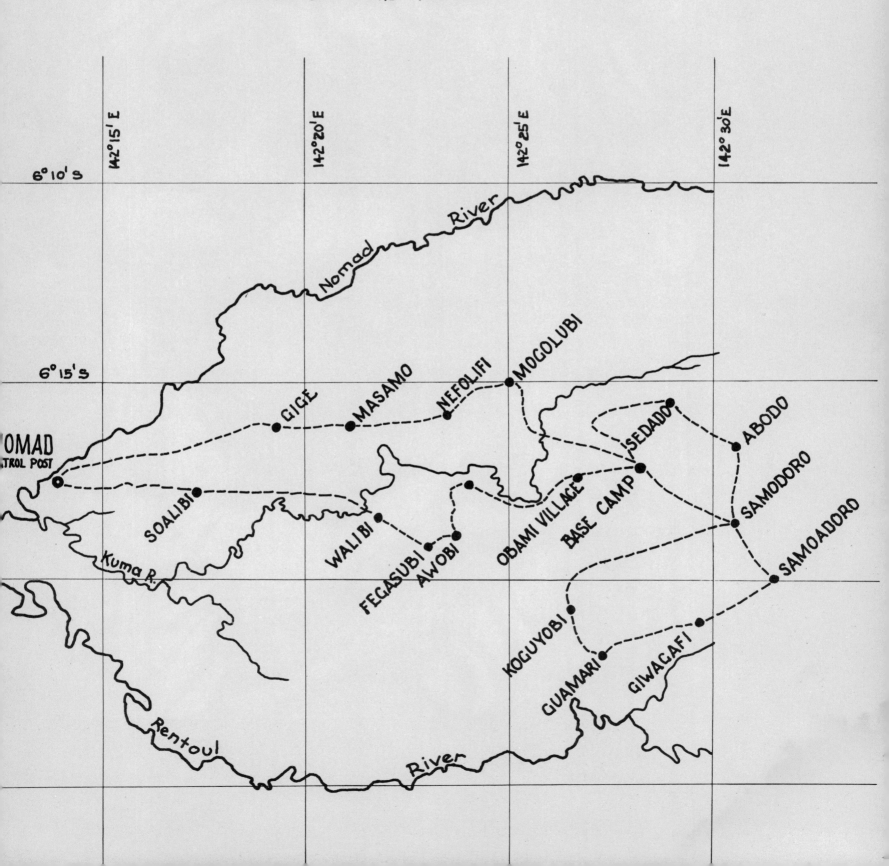

PATROL MAP

BIAMI AREA

----- Route taken by
Anderson-Wells Patrol.

142°15' E

142°20' E

142°25' E

142°30' E

6°10' S

6°15' S

Nomad River

NOMAD PATROL POST

Kuma R.

Rentoul River

GIGE

MASAMO

NEFOLIFI

MOGOLUBI

ISEDADO

ABODO

SAMODORO

SAMOADORO

SOALIBI

WALIBI

FEGASUBI

AWOBI

OBAMI VILLAGE

BASE CAMP

KOGUYOBI

GUAMARI

GIWACAFI